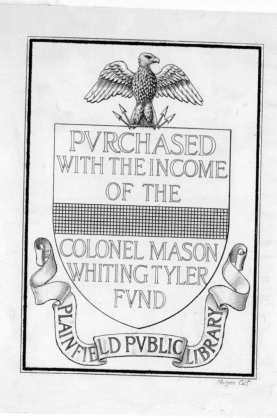

PVRCHASED
WITH THE INCOME
OF THE

COLONEL MASON
WHITING TYLER
FVND

PLAINFIELD PVBLIC LIBRARY

Morgan Coll.

Consciousness in Concord

Consciousness in Concord

The Text of Thoreau's Hitherto "Lost Journal"
(1840–1841)
Together with Notes and a Commentary

by

PERRY MILLER

1 9 5 8

The Riverside Press Cambridge

HOUGHTON MIFFLIN COMPANY   BOSTON

FOR
ARCHIBALD AND ADA MACLEISH

Acknowledgments

ONE OF THE compensations of scholarship is the obligations a student is privileged to acquire.

I am first of all grateful to the Pierpont Morgan Library, of New York City, for granting me the rare opportunity of presenting to the world a segment of Henry Thoreau's *Journal.* The Library added to the weight of my indebtedness by lending every assistance to the operation. I am especially obligated to Mr. Herbert Cahoon, Curator of Autograph Manuscripts, whose knowledge of Thoreau (as of so much else) is immense, and who always put his erudition at my disposal.

I thank the Houghton Library of Harvard University for permission to use and quote from its collection of Thoreau manuscripts (MS. Am. 278.5).

I am particularly grateful to the Henry E. Huntington Library and Art Gallery, of San Marino, California, for permission to read and to quote from the microfilm of the fragmentary *Journal* of 1842 to 1850 (HM 13182). Over and above this, I express my thanks to Professor Kenneth W. Cameron, of Trinity College, who is preparing the full text of this fascinating document and who handsomely waived his prior rights to allow me to quote some six or seven passages.

The Henry W. and Albert A. Berg Collection of the New York Public Library granted me permission to quote from the letters of Isaiah Williams and to reproduce the two invaluable letters of Thoreau to him.

Acknowledgments

The Ralph Waldo Emerson Memorial Association kindly permits me to quote the passage on friendship from Emerson's original and unpublished *Journals*.

Every student of Thoreau (or of American Literature in the period) finds himself deeply in debt to Professor Walter Harding, editor of *The Thoreau Society Bulletin*. In this case, my indebtedness is both general and specific, for Professor Harding read my transcript of volume 3 and gave me unstintingly the benefit of his massive scholarship.

Elizabeth Williams Miller worked with me throughout the often difficult transcription, and the equally bothersome commentary.

I trust I need not insist, though I shall, that responsibility for any errors, either in transcription or in statement of fact, which may be proved upon me is my own.

The young Thoreau said it well, and prophetically, on January 8, 1842:

> One cannot too soon forget his errors and misdemeanors; for [to] dwell long upon them is to add to the offense, and repentance and sorrow can only be displaced by somewhat better, and which is as free and original as if they had not been.

PERRY MILLER

Harvard University
August 31, 1957

References

In order to avoid what in a work of this sort would become a cumbersome apparatus (not to say an impertinence) of footnotes, I have placed such references at the back of the book.

All citations from the *Writings* of Henry Thoreau are out of the Walden Edition (Boston: Houghton Mifflin and Company, 1906). For the sake of clarity I give the titles of the volumes of writings rather than numbers, and for the *Journal* use the subsidiary numbers of that work rather than the overall numbers of the edition. For brevity's sake I abbreviate *A Week on the Concord and Merrimack Rivers* to *Week* and volumes of the *Journal* to *J.*

For the two essays of this period which never appeared in the Walden Edition, I use *The Service*, edited by F. B. Sanborn (Boston: Charles E. Goodspeed, 1902), and *Sir Walter Raleigh*, introduction by F. B. Sanborn, edited by Henry Aiken Metcalf (Boston: The Bibliophile Society, 1905).

References to the published writings of Emerson are to the Houghton Mifflin edition of 1903–1904; for his *Journals*, to the standard edition (Edward Waldo Emerson and Waldo Emerson Forbes, Houghton Mifflin, 1909–1914); for his letters, to *The Letters of Ralph Waldo Emerson*, edited by Ralph L. Rusk (New York: Columbia University Press, 1939).

In the hope of avoiding confusion, I make specific references to numbers of the Walden Edition of the *Journal* by capitalizing "Volume." Thoreau numbered the volumes of his manuscript simply 1, 2, 3, etc. To make clear when I am referring to one of these, I keep to the lower case: e.g., ours is "volume 3."

In printing the text of volume 3 I have affixed as footnotes my comments and indications of the uses Thoreau elsewhere made of the material. All observations on purely textual alterations or experiments he performed within these pages are described in "Notes on Textual Variants" at the end of the book.

In these years — and indeed in the 1850's — Thoreau endeavored to keep his bound volumes of manuscript in such neat form, with numbered pages, that they might go easily (as ultimately they did) to a printer. But once he had a volume in his hands, he could seldom resist the impulse to make odd jottings on the lining covers or on the flyleaves (he always preserved a leaf for this function). Hence my transcript begins with the notations on the front cover lining and on the two sides of the flyleaf (p. 133) and commences with the actual text of volume 3, as he designed it, only on page 135, with the gnomic verse. This he calls page 1. Likewise, I conclude the printing with the miscellaneous notes he made on the last flyleaf and on the back cover lining.

Contents

PART I

Introduction

1

"A Journal,

of No Very Wide Circulation"

IN 1909 Stephen H. Wakeman sold to J. Pierpont Morgan a yellow pine box containing thirty-eight manuscript notebooks of Henry Thoreau. According to legend, the box was carpentered by Thoreau himself. He must have constructed it in his last year, when his health was ruined. Yet even on the brink of the grave Thoreau could do, as he always had done, a precise job; he clearly intended to bind up physically this central product of his life. Hence it did seem strange that the books fitted their case a bit loosely.

However, these notebooks apparently comprised all of the extant *Journal* — all, that is, which had been preserved by the writer known to fame as the author of *Walden*. They were all that had appeared in the Walden Edition prepared by Bradford Torrey (with the assistance of Francis H. Allen), published by Houghton Mifflin and Company in 1906. From these manuscripts Torrey and Allen produced fourteen volumes of printed text. Bound uniformly with them were the two books Thoreau managed to get published in his lifetime — *A Week on the Concord and Merrimack Rivers* (1849) and *Walden* (1854) — together with the four volumes of essays, lectures, poems, travel sketches, and posthumously printed pieces that had supposedly received their final form in the Riverside Edition of 1893.

Thus the twenty volumes of 1906 could claim to be "definitive." They add up to something over two million words, a massive production, indeed, for a man who died at forty-four.

Introduction

No doubt, so expensive a publishing venture would not have been undertaken had Thoreau not written *Walden*, or had Ticknor and Fields not issued it at Boston, in August 1854. Torrey and Allen did their yeomen's labor on the *Journal*, persuaded that its fourteen volumes were justified by this one book. Had there been no *Walden*, Henry Thoreau, even as the author of a fourteen-volume *Journal* of the Transcendental epoch, would have been rated in 1906 for what his contemporaries thought him: a minor satellite of Ralph Waldo Emerson.

Beyond doubt, *Walden* made the difference. Because of it, Thoreau loomed, even at the end of his century, as a major writer within the Transcendental fellowship. Because of *Walden*, there was an excuse for bringing out in 1906 *all* of his *Journal*. (Even so, many then thought that the chief function of the Walden Edition would be to prod the owners of Emerson's *Journals* into publication — as indeed it did, in 1911.)

Since 1906 the stature of Thoreau as writer has steadily increased. Since 1906 there has also grown a realization that his *Journal*, apart from any relation to *Walden*, is a unique creation. It can be listed along with certain other by-the-way achievements, such as Emerson's *Journals* or the collected letters of Henry Adams or Henry James (or more pertinently with the poetry of Emily Dickinson). But only of Thoreau's private discourse can we say that the monologue is, granting a few improvisations, a deliberately constructed work of art, in no respect subsidiary to the artist's public appearances.

In the revolutions of time, Thoreau's elaborately oblique reference to the then unpublished, and obviously unpublishable, *Journal* takes on a somber tone. When he mentioned it in *Walden*,[1] he was writing out of ironic acceptance of failure: today, the irony turns upon himself, and extenuates the braggadocio of his first chapter:

4

"A Journal, of No Very Wide Circulation"

> For a long time I was reporter to a journal, of no
> very wide circulation, whose editor has never yet seen fit
> to print the bulk of my contributions, and, as is too
> common with writers, I got only my labor for my pains.
> However, in this case my pains were their own reward.

In all the literature of the world, here is the case of a sensible
man who found nobody so interesting to talk with as himself.

However, Thoreau's *Journal* takes on this self-intoxicated
— this self-infatuated — character only with Volume II of the
Torrey edition, which opens with May of 1850. By then,
Thoreau had acknowledged, even to himself, that his one
published venture, the *Week* (brought out under terms dis-
advantageous to himself, by James Munroe in May 1849),
was a failure — so far as any popular reception was concerned.
In this spring of 1850 he had on his table an almost completed (he then thought it completed) manuscript called
Walden, for which neither he nor his patron Emerson could
find a publisher. Furthermore, by this dismal spring, it was
clear that, though he had made valiant efforts, he would
never, like Emerson, earn a living by delivering "lectures."
Thoreau was perforce reduced to testing the validity of a
proclamation he had gaily released in July of 1840: "Methinks
I hear the clarion sound, and the clang of corselet and buckler
from many a silent hamlet of the soul" (see below, p. 143).
Though he never wore a corselet nor hefted a buckler, he was
sentenced to making literature, the best he could, out of the
clarion and clang of his "silent" hamlet. From May of 1850
until the last moment in which he had the strength to put
down a sentence — until the struggle on November 3, 1861,
to make prose out of the dance of a kitten and the (haunt-
ingly) stratified furrows of gravel along the railroad cut — the
Journal is a sustained oratorio, varied with arias, trios, and
with thematic recapitulations. While *Walden* was awaiting
a publisher, between 1850 and 1854, several motifs in the

5

Journal were added to that manuscript; at the end of the decade, still hoping to win an audience, Thoreau would search through it for essays which, after his death, his sister and friends could furnish *The Atlantic Monthly*. Nevertheless, in substance these Volumes II to XIV of the Walden Edition are a deliberate accretion, essentially indivisible, consciously designed — as much so as, let us say, the accumulations of a Marcel Proust — to be their own excuse for being.

But, let us be clear: this characterization does not apply to the *Journal* material before 1850. Of this record, Torrey and Allen printed everything available in 1906 as Volume I. They found, starting at the left edge of the pine box, five notebooks — the sort that Thoreau bought in the village store for a few cents apiece — filled with entries, generally in ink, from October 22, 1837, to April 13, 1842. Thoreau numbered the first ones 1 and 2; volume 2 ends with July 27, 1840, and the matter of these makes up pages 1 to 172 of Torrey's Volume I. The remaining three bear Thoreau's numbering — 4, 5, 6 — and these supply pages 173 to 360 of Volume I.

Torrey did not have the booklet which Thoreau numbered volume 3, dated July 30, 1840, to January 22, 1841. As Francis Allen later said, when it did turn up, had he and Torrey known that it existed, they would have printed it between the present pages 172 and 173 of the *Journal*, Volume I in the Walden Edition.

Thoreau's pine box was bequeathed to his sister Sophia. She was as crotchety a creature as any of the Thoreaus; she cordially hated Henry's erstwhile friends, the younger William Ellery Channing and Franklin B. Sanborn. She died in 1876, pointedly leaving the box to the one being who, during Thoreau's existence, professed to be a disciple, Harrison Gray Otis Blake of Worcester.

From 1881 to 1892, Blake inaccurately culled passages out of the manuscript, and so printed four volumes; two of these,

"A Journal, of No Very Wide Circulation"

Winter (1888) and *Autumn* (1892), bowdlerized entries from notebook volume 3. We assume that it was then in his hands.

Blake left the box to Edward Harlow Russell of Worcester; while it was in Russell's hands, Bradford Torrey made his transcripts. He found no volume 3: the obvious inference is that Blake mislaid it. This hypothesis accords with everything we know about the irresponsibility of Harrison Blake.

In 1905 Russell sold the box to George S. Hellman, who in turn sold it to Stephen H. Wakeman. After Wakeman transferred his collection to the J. Pierpont Morgan Library, volume 3 appeared on the market. In 1912 Mr. Wakeman bought it; at the sale of his library it went to Mr. Warren H. Colson. In 1956 it was acquired by the Morgan Library, a gift of the Fellows, with the special assistance of Mr. C. Waller Barrett, Mrs. Louis M. Rabinowitz and Mr. Robert H. Taylor. It was found to fit snugly into the box, thus proving that even in his last extremity Henry Thoreau's eye had not lost its perception nor his hand its cunning: he built the case for precisely these thirty-nine volumes; and now these fill it.

2

The Biographical Provenience

"Says I to myself" should be the motto of my journal.
(November 11, 1851; J, III, 107)

As HENRY THOREAU makes his first notation in volume 3 of the manuscript *Journal*, he has just become twenty-three: he was born in Concord on July 12, 1817.

The paternal grandfather came from the Isle of Jersey. The father — a dim, inarticulate figure — failed in several undertakings until in 1823 he began to make a modest income out of the manufacture of pencils in his shed. (Henry's *Journal* conceals the hours he spent helping in this business, as also, after the father's death, February 3, 1859, the extent to which he carried it on.) The mother, Cynthia Dunbar Thoreau, came of Yankee and Scots families, and was famed as the most rapid — we might say, compulsive — talker in all Concord. She contributed to the family income by conducting a genteel boardinghouse. Two Thoreau aunts, Maria and Jane, lived intermittently in this house, along with Henry's older sister, Helen (in frail health; she would die in June 1849), and a younger one, Sophia — homely, eager, a lover of "Nature" in the lush vein of giftbook sentimentalism. One fact incontestably emerges: the home was under oppressive female domination.

In 1840 — all during volume 3 — Henry still has by his side his invaluable masculine ally: brother John, two years older than he. John was genial, gay; Henry worshiped him.

This Yankee-Huguenot family had been unable to send

John to college, but managed by stringent economies to put Henry through Harvard. After four years of undistinguished study, Henry was graduated at Cambridge on August 16, 1837, taking part in a colloquy on "The Commercial Spirit" in which he pleaded with Americans to toil only one day a week and to spend the other six in the widespread garden, drinking in "the soft influences and sublime revelations of Nature." [1] At a time when any American boy with a college degree — despite the Panic of 1837 — could be fairly certain of commercial success, Thoreau voluntarily returned to the femininity of his "home" in Concord. In 1838 he and John organized a private school.

During the months of this volume, Henry is happily teaching alongside his brother, his days fully occupied. About this activity there is, neither in this volume nor in the preceding two, any hint.

It appears that in 1837 Emerson's attention was called to the propensity of Henry Thoreau to entertain thoughts similar to those he himself had. We guess that Thoreau had read Emerson's *Nature*, published in 1836, and even that he heard Emerson deliver "The American Scholar" as the Phi Beta Kappa address at Harvard on August 7, 1837. He opens volume 1 of the *Journal* with a cryptic paragraph:

> Oct. 22 [1837] "what are you doing now?" he asked. "Do you keep a journal?" So I make my first entry to-day.

We are bound to cast Emerson as "he," even though we have learned not to assume that this is really the first "entry." By the next February 11, 1838, Emerson could note in his own diary, reflecting on the boy's performance at an evening discussion, "I delight much in my young friend, who seems to have as free and erect a mind as any I have ever met." [2] By the end of that year, observers were remarking how Thoreau was copying Emerson's manners of speech, even how his nose had become Emersonian.

On the cover lining of our volume, Thoreau admires the "sage" who could hold up one finger to express individuality, and two for dualism, without injuring the effect of his action by speaking: this seems to be the restrained gesticulation which Emerson made into histrionic art. On page 211 of this manuscript, and again on the back cover, Thoreau is working out the observation that some persons — especially "my friend" — present different aspects in their separate profiles. Admirers of Emerson were beginning to note, as finally the sculptor Daniel French was emphatically to say, that the two sides of Emerson's face were strangely unlike. We guess, therefore, that in volume 3 young Henry is still captivated by the image of Emerson.

Possibly because of Emerson's backing, Thoreau gave his first public lecture, on "Society," before the Concord Lyceum, April 11, 1838.

In the spring of 1839, eleven-year-old Edmund Sewall, whose home was in Scituate, attended the brothers' school. On June 24 Henry copied into volume 1 a poem addressed to Edmund (without naming him), entitled "Sympathy." In July 1839, Edmund's sister, Ellen Devereaux Sewall, aged seventeen, visited Concord; probably she resided in Mrs. Thoreau's boardinghouse. John and Henry may have gone to Scituate in December 1839. In June 1840, just as this volume commences, Ellen was again in Concord. We know that Henry took her rowing on the river, June 19. As the story goes, in this August John proposed to her, she briefly accepted him, then quickly declined. She is said to have refused Henry's offer of marriage in November. In 1844 she married the Reverend Joseph Osgood of Scituate, bore him several children, and lived a happy life.

The Biographical Provenience

Early in July, just as these entries begin, Emerson and Margaret Fuller were bringing out, after months of travail, the first number of The Dial. Emerson is on record as inspired, among other motives, with the dream that the magazine would become a vehicle for his young genius. "My Henry Thoreau," he wrote to his brother on September 26, 1839, "will be a great poet for such a company, & one of these days for all companies." [3] However, the managing editor, Margaret, was less enthusiastic: she is not mentioned in this volume (in fact, throughout the Journal she is mentioned as little as possible), but she is very much there. She did not like Henry's verses, and she positively refused the two prose essays Thoreau worked up during the spring and summer of 1840 in confident expectation that The Dial would publish them — "The Service" (see below, pp. 136–138, for Margaret's treatment of it) and "Sir Walter Raleigh." (The Service would not be printed until Sanborn edited it in 1902, and Sir Walter Raleigh not until 1905; neither of these appears in the Walden Edition, but there is no comprehending the young Thoreau without a reading of them.)

In spite of Miss Fuller's objection, the first number of The Dial, coming out in July 1840, did usher Thoreau into the world of letters, though in no way to call attention to him. On page 71 it carried his poem to the "gentle boy," which was signed "T." On page 117 it printed his unsigned piece, "Aulus Persius Flaccus." This is more translation and compilation than original essay, such as he was attempting in "The Service," and is a slight enough performance at best. But behind it there was, by July, a story, and that story is of importance to him who would understand Henry Thoreau.

He submitted his first draft to Emerson in March 1840;[4] the great man was delighted with it, until Margaret riddled it with her criticisms. Young Thoreau at first responded with the traditional truculence of insulted genius: he told Emerson,

who on April 15 repeated the message to Margaret, that he
had too mean an opinion of "Persius" and of anything else
he had written "to care to revise them but he will give us
Persius as it is, if we will do the revising." [5] Within a few
days, as we should expect, Thoreau ate his humble pie: he took
the essay home to do his own correcting.[6] Margaret consented,
with a conspicuous lack of enthusiasm, to run it in the first
number: she had praise only for the motto Emerson affixed
to it;[7] but even so, it went back to Henry for still another re-
vision.[8] This was a more rigorous tuition than Thoreau had
received at Harvard College, and we can imagine how it galled
him. But the ultimate annoyance came when he opened the
first number of *The Dial* and found that Emerson, in copying
out "Sympathy," had ruined one of his couplets. Thoreau had
written,

> For walls and ports do only serve alway
> For a pretence to feebleness and sin.

His mentor had grandly put "posts" in the place of "ports,"
and so wrecked Thoreau's meaning.[9]

Undeterred by this (to us) shocking mismanagement,
Emerson went on supervising the boy's verses: "we must mend
him if we can," he tells Margaret on July 27.[10] We measure
the sublimity of Emerson's insensitivity when we find him
amazed on August 4 to discover that Henry "boggled" at
Margaret's suggestion that he use "relumes" instead of "doth
have" in what we, I am sure, consider one of his better lines:
"Nature doth have her dawn each day." "But our tough
Yankee," Emerson deduces, "must have his tough verse." [11]
Clearly Emerson is acting out of the utmost loyalty to Henry
Thoreau; but the drama is going on behind the pages of this
innocent-seeming volume of the *Journal*. When Theodore
Parker came for a day's visit to Concord, on August 10, Emer-

son sweetly expressed his admiration for the "Persius" — which Parker thought simply "foolish." ("I hope," said the least transcendental of the Transcendentalists, "he will write for the newspapers more & less for the Dial. I would recommend him to the editor of the New World to keep the youth out of mischief.")[12] Henry Thoreau must have known, more or less, what was being said about him, and tightened his lips; when he put together his first book, into the *Week* he defiantly inserted the complete text of "Aulus Persius Flaccus."[13]

Strangely — though sadly? — our manuscript observes on the first of January 1841 that "Friendship" is in *The Dial* (it gives the date December 28), and on January 16 notes that "Sic Vita" is also in the magazine. "Friendship," with its arresting apostrophe, "Let such pure hate still underprop/Our love," did not in fact appear there until October 1841, while "Sic Vita" (announcing "I am a parcel of vain strivings tied/By a chance bond together") came in the July number. We know that in this autumn and winter Thoreau was assisting Emerson with the editorial chores, and so he may, on the dates here mentioned, have got Emerson's consent for future printing. (Even though a contributor and an unpaid clerk, Thoreau handed over money to become a subscriber.)[14] Conduct of the magazine was monumentally inefficient; possibly merely mechanical delays rather than Margaret's hostility account for the belated appearances of Thoreau's verses. However, we can decipher that the poems were a focus of his creative endeavor in the months of this *Journal*; we can assume further that his mind is running much upon *The Dial*, though the manuscript of volume 3 gives it little mention.

In December 1840, Brook Farm had been organized and Emerson was asked to join — on the assumption that, if anybody did, he certainly should. Instead, he entered into his *Journals* the much quoted determination not to raise the siege of his hen-coop to march off to a pretended siege of Babylon;

to a grievously disappointed George Ripley on December 15 he explained that it seemed to him circuitous and operose "to put on your community the task of my emancipation which I ought to take on myself." [15] In Concord, he said, he had builded, and "I cannot accuse my townsmen or my social position of my domestic grievances: — only my own sloth & conformity." There is no indication that Ripley counted on Thoreau as a potential recruit; volume 3 utterly ignores the fanfaronade this adventure was exciting among apostles of the "Newness," but it is worth wondering whether Emerson explained to his neophyte the reasons for his refusal.

On January 27, 1841, five days after volume 3 is finished, Henry and John Thoreau together maintained the affirmative in a "debate" at the Concord Lyceum on a set question: "Is it ever proper to offer forcible resistance?" Their opponent was Bronson Alcott! [16]

The presence of Alcott (whom on October 7 Emerson calls "the majestic egotist")[17] in the background of this volume must be remembered, even though he is specifically mentioned only once, on August 14, as being the classical extreme in opposition to the Scythian barbarism of George Minot. Minott (with the second "t" properly affixed to his name) becomes a vivid character in the later *Journal*, reappearing in October 1851,[18] as "the most poetical farmer," who takes infinite satisfaction in his labor, whose farming has ever been an amusement that lasted him longer than gunning and fishing. In here raising up Minott as the antithesis to Alcott, Thoreau gives us leave to surmise that Minott also was an "influence" throughout the decade of 1840 to 1850. But more importantly, Alcott makes his bow in a *Journal* in which he is later to figure as an object of admiration and ridicule — the most hospitable intellect, Thoreau would note after Alcott visited him at the Pond, of any man living, who could embrace high and low: "For children," Henry would revealingly add, "how much that means, for the insane and vagabond, for the poet and scholar." [19]

In 1840, Henry has not yet categorized his heroes as children, the insane, vagabonds, poets and scholars. He is still dreaming the melodramatics of "The Service"; he has not yet become the persistent vagabond of the 1850's, returning to his *Journal* "from going to and fro in the earth, and from walking up and down in it." He could not understand, though he might admire, the ordeal Alcott had suffered (tried even as had been Job) in the failure of the school in Boston. But here Alcott was, Plato incarnate, come to Concord in March of 1840. The entry of August 14 shows that Thoreau had already been conversing with him. (Possibly it is Alcott rather than Emerson who held up one finger for individuality and two for dualism?) At any rate, with Emerson, Minott, Alcott in town during the summer of 1840 — not to mention the cyclonic descents of Margaret Fuller — young Henry was not lacking instructors. The scanting of their names in the manuscript is proof positive of how much he was learning from them.

Alcott and his family settled in the "Hosmer Cottage," west of the town, facing the river, and there Abby May was born on July 28. Bronson was happy to have Emerson for a neighbor, but even he was aghast upon realizing the seclusion to which he had brought himself. He wrote his brother, "I have even wished some portion of the gifts with which I have been blessed had been withheld, if I might thereby have been brought into closer sympathy with the ordinary pursuits of mankind." [20] To be instructed by a philosopher who could not only appreciate his own endowments but who could also envy the occupation of a George Minott was excitement enough. Particularly because in this summer of 1840, the Plato of New England was earning the little income his family could bank on by day-labor in the fields. Labor, Alcott was insisting on July 29, supplies man with primeval dignity: "Sloth is the tempter that beguiles, and casts him out of his Paradise of innocency." [21] Of Alcott, the great William Ellery Channing, Unitarian "bishop" of all theological liberals, wrote in 1841 to Elizabeth Peabody: "Orpheus at the plough is after my own heart; there he teaches a grand lesson, — more than most of us teach by the pen." We know not whether Thoreau ever saw Miss Peabody's printing of Channing's letter. Even if he did, long before he could have studied it, Thoreau had taken unto himself the title of Apollo chained to the plow of King Admetus; through his *Journal* he rings changes on the theme. Wherefore, he beheld in Alcott a portent.

In 1843 Alcott refused to pay his taxes, was arrested by the constable of Concord, Sam Staples, who in bewilderment confessed that Alcott seemed to be moved by "principle." In that year Alcott also undertook to bring Utopia to earth by establishing his colony at "Fruitlands," in Harvard, Massachusetts. It was clear to him, as it had seemed clear in 1840, that "on a survey of the present civilized world, Providence seems to have ordained the United States of America, more especially New England, as the field wherein this idea is to be realized in actual experience." [22] Rivals for the role of Apollo might love each other, but get in each other's way: just before the Alcotts entered upon their disastrous experiment, in February 1843, Bronson accused Henry of making an idol out of Nature, and Henry replied that Alcott was so deficient in the faculty of appreciating Nature he could not judge of it.[23] The moral may be — as this volume 3 shows it had already become — that the experiment of reviving Eden in New England must of necessity be conducted through a love of Nature, not of family.

By January 1841, when this volume ends, John's health was failing. On April 1 the school was closed. On April 26 Thoreau took up his two-year residence in Emerson's house, as general handyman and editorial assistant.

On January 11, 1842, John Thoreau died of lockjaw. Henry's *Journal*, bursting with thoughts up to January 9, is silent between that date and February 19, when it resumes with, "I never saw two men sufficiently great to meet as two." [24] The sixth volume of the manuscript *Journal* ends on April 3, 1842.

Emerson assumed the editing of *The Dial* in the spring of 1842, the first under his direction being the issue for July. In this appears Thoreau's first prose composition — discounting the derivative "Aulus Persius Flaccus." Ostensibly a review of state documents (see below, p. 166), "Natural History of Massachusetts" draws upon the six volumes of manuscript *Journal*. In the next years, 1842–1844, Emerson gave Thoreau all the space he could fill. Henry drew further upon the *Journal*, as he also did for pieces in *The Boston Miscellany* ("A Walk to Wachusett," January 1843) and in *The Democratic Review* ("The Landlord," October 1843, and "Paradise (To Be) Regained," November 1843).

On May 1, 1843, Thoreau went — at Emerson's insistence — to live with William Emerson on Staten Island. In November, desolate with homesickness, he came back to Concord. In the spring of 1845 he built his hut beside Walden Pond; he formally occupied it on July 4. He left it on September 6, 1847.

At the Pond, besides raising beans and reading the *Bhagavad-Gita*, Thoreau worked on the *Week*. Constructed around a voyage he had taken with John in 1839, the book is an accretion of his decade of "journalizing," defying both Emerson and Margaret Fuller by reprinting his *Dial* verses and "Aulus Persius Flaccus." The book was finished by 1847; Emerson tried to market it, but four publishers refused. Thoreau worked on it through 1848, and finally paid Munroe to produce it in May 1849, in an edition of one thousand copies. In 1853 Munroe shipped him the seven hundred and six unsold volumes. Thoreau stored these in his attic, and then confided to his *Journal* one of his renowned sentences (considering what price today a first edition of the *Week* will fetch): "I have now a library of nearly nine hundred volumes, over seven hundred of which I wrote myself." [25]

Walden, ready for publication in 1849, was not accepted by Ticknor and Fields until 1854. Even then, the publishers made no money on it.

This "lost" volume of Thoreau's *Journal* is a brief but essential episode in what to the young man of Concord was a rush of experience. To interpret its gnomic utterances we have to consider it primarily as it figures in his literary apprenticeship, second, as it relates to his biography, and third, for what it, along with cognate writings, reveals about the character of Thoreau's mind.

3

The Method

It is remarkable what a curse seems to attach to any place
which has long been inhabited by man. Vermin of various
kinds abide with him. (September 22, 1859; *J*, XII, 340)

SINCE VOLUME 3 is an integral part of the initial six, it
can hardly be discussed separately. With the complete record
(to the extent Thoreau was pleased to make it) of 1837 to
1842 reunited, we can for the first time think coherently about
the literary apprenticeship of Henry Thoreau.

However, we must note that Thoreau did not abruptly cease
"journalizing" on April 3, 1842, with the end of volume 6.
Torrey and Allen had a fragmentary notebook for 1845–1846,
probably kept while Thoreau was at the Pond (they print this
as pages 361–402 of *Journal*, Volume I). They also had a
mutilated collection of items, mostly undated, which they as-
cribed to 1845–1847 (pp. 403–437) and a "commonplace
book," presumably filled before 1847, from which Thoreau
obviously drew in composing the *Week* (pp. 438–488).[1]

After the Walden Edition, collectors, libraries, scholarly
sleuths nosed about for Thoreau material. We are now as-
sured that he kept at least one systematic journal in 1842 and
1843 (pieces of this are in the Houghton Library, Harvard
University), and another from September 24, 1843, to January 7, 1844 (fragments of this are now in the Huntington
Library, HM 13182). The latter has annotations by Sanborn,
and in part is printed in his *The First and Last Journeys of
Thoreau* (Boston, 1905). Sanborn says that Thoreau himself

tore up the volume, and we can assume that he likewise
wrecked his other manuscripts between 1842 and 1850.

This volume, of the autumn of 1843, was evidently begun
on Staten Island. An early page, another of his many efforts
to define the function of the poet, concludes:

> He records a moment of pure life. Who can see these
> cities and say that there is any life in them? I walked
> through New York yesterday — and met no real or
> living person.[2]

There endures also a cover for another notebook which
Thoreau probably wrote at the Pond, the index of which shows
that it once held matter incorporated into both books. While
generally the narrative of *Walden* is put in the past tense, there
are striking shifts to the present, often in the middle of a
paragraph. For sixteen days Thoreau "saw" the workmen
harvesting ice from the pond: "now they are all gone, and in
thirty days more, probably, I shall look from the same window
on the pure sea-green Walden water there. . . ."[3] These
alternations appear studied; we detect behind them the
existence of a notebook composed mainly in the present tense.

Still, whatever the kind or kinds of journals Thoreau kept
between April 3, 1842, and the spring of 1850, they all went
into the hopper of his creative operation. They were disem-
boweled and cannibalized. Odds and ends of work-sheets also
remain — enough to show either that he did his revisions on
pages of an eviscerated journal or upon pages copied from a
journal manuscript. We see that this process went on
ferociously, that many portions have been subjected to a dozen
recastings.

However, though he later made use of about half the entries
in the first six volumes, these books he never physically pulled
apart. Sometimes, as our passages show, he worked over a
paragraph, revising his original ink with a pencil, but whatever

of these volumes he ultimately used, he copied. Only after the
Week was published, after most of *Walden* was written (but
unpublished!), did Henry Thoreau find himself isolated, con-
fronting the defeat of his high anticipation; only then would
he turn to the *Journal* as the confessedly main concern of his
being. What in the early 1840's he had taken for granted, in
1845 he could at last explain:

> From all points of the compass, from the earth beneath
> and the heavens above, have come these inspirations
> and been entered duly in the order of their arrival in
> the journal. Thereafter, when the time arrived, they
> were winnowed into lectures, and again, in due time,
> from lectures into essays. And at last they stand, like
> the cubes of Pythagoras, firmly on either basis; like
> statues on their pedestals, but the statues rarely take
> hold of hands. There is only such connection and
> series as is attainable in the galleries.[4]

Here was the challenge: to make of his galleries (he knew of
European galleries only by hearsay) something more organic
than an assemblage of items. He could foresee the problem,
but in the 1840's was certain he could surmount it: "And this
affects their immediate practical and popular influence."
     It is a long, an anguished cry from this nervous assurance to
the resignation of, for instance, October 21, 1857:

> Is not the poet bound to write his own biography? Is
> there any other work for him but a good journal? We
> do not wish to know how his imaginary hero, but how
> he, the actual hero, lived from day to day.[5]

Between volume 3 (and the essay on Raleigh) and such an
effort at self-consolation came the enervating struggle. In
August 1851, as he was realizing just how narrowly he was
pinioned, he could observe, "It takes a man of genius to travel

in his own country, in his native village." [6] In 1840 he had already become the traveler in Concord, but with every intention (as "The Service" reveals) of gathering material for a hero as stupendous as Don Juan. On February 8, 1841, he imaged himself a clerk in the counting-room of the gods, "and at evening transfer the account from day-book to ledger." He could not think of the divine ledger as something shut up in his desk: "It is papyrus by the riverside; it is vellum in the pastures; it is parchment on the hills." [7] The crow, the goose, the eagle must carry his quill, but it matters not if his imagination does not soar, even if it gropes in slime and mud, for "then I write with a reed." In the ecstasy of this time he was sure nothing could hinder him; his scrawls, he all but shouted, touch upon accidents as cosmic as earthquake or eclipse: "Upland and lowland, forest and field have been ransacked."

Even amid these assurances, however, there were already puzzlements. "Of all strange and unaccountable things this journalizing is the strangest," he mused on January 29, 1841. [8] Sometimes he wondered if he cluttered his counter with homemade stuffs, but was delighted to find, on looking over his entries, that he really wrote better than he knew: "and what perhaps seemed a festoon of dried apple or pumpkin will prove a string of Brazilian diamonds, or pearls from Coromandel."

Perhaps the chief reason why he never ripped these volumes to shreds was that he wanted to discover what they would sound like after he had more experience with writing. They would be eloquent to him, beyond even the richest pages of later volumes, because — sparse, even crabbed as they are — they radiated hope. By 1856 he would berate himself that too often he let his *Journal* become (as he held Emerson wantonly allowed his to become) a preserve of things well done or said instead of a record of experiences and growth. "The charm of the journal," he then pleaded with himself, "must consist